AMAZING SPORTS

BASEBALL

BY LORI DITTMER

CREATIVE EDUCATION • CREATIVE PAPERBACKS

Published by Creative Education and Creative Paperbacks
P.O. Box 227, Mankato, Minnesota 56002
Creative Education and Creative Paperbacks are imprints of
The Creative Company
www.thecreativecompany.us

Design by The Design Lab
Production by Dana Koehler
Art direction by Rita Marshall
Printed in the United States of America

Photographs by Alamy (Juice Images), iStockphoto (kreicher),
Newscom (BILL GREENBLATT/UPI, Kyodo, Kenneth K. Lam/TNS,
Nhat V. Meyer/TNS), Shutterstock (Aspen Photo, Brocreative,
DJTaylor, Margie Hurwich, JoeSAPhotos, Richard Paul Kane, KoQ
Creative, Joseph Sohm)

Library of Congress Cataloging-in-Publication Data
Names: Dittmer, Lori, author.
Title: Baseball / Lori Dittmer.
Series: Amazing sports.
Includes index.
Summary: Get the ball rolling with this high-interest introduction to
baseball, the sport known for its bats and bases. Also included is a
biographical story about professional baseball player Ichiro Suzuki.

Identifiers:
ISBN 978-1-64026-211-9 (hardcover)
ISBN 978-1-62832-774-8 (pbk)
ISBN 978-1-64000-346-0 (eBook)
This title has been submitted for CIP processing under LCCN
2019937892.

First Edition HC 9 8 7 6 5 4 3 2 1
First Edition PBK 9 8 7 6 5 4 3 2 1

Table of Contents

Games like baseball have been played for more than 200 years! In 1845, a group of men in New York City made a list of rules. The game of baseball that we know today was born.

An early rule ended the practice of throwing a ball at a runner to get him out.

Players use a small round ball and a long bat. Each player in the field wears a padded glove with a pocket to catch the ball. The batter wears a helmet. A hard rubber or canvas bag marks each base.

Batting helmets help keep the batter's head safe from being hit by a pitch.

The infield is the area inside the four bases. From above, it looks diamond-shaped. In the center of the infield is the pitcher's mound. The outfield goes beyond the infield. Foul lines mark where the ball goes out of bounds.

Many parks have foul poles that mark the edges of the field of play.

A baseball game is split into nine innings. The teams take turns hitting the ball each inning. A turn is over after three outs.

The pitcher throws the ball to the batter, and outfielders (above) try to catch hits.

A player who makes it to first base is said to have hit a single.

Players try to get on base.
Once someone rounds all the bases, the team scores a run. Sometimes, a batter hits a **home run**. The team with the most runs at the end of the game wins.

home run a hit that enables the batter to make a complete lap of the bases and score a run

The manager leads the team. There are nine positions at play. Three outfielders try to catch the ball in the air or scoop it up from the ground. One player is at each base, trying to get runners out.

A fielder holding the ball while touching the base can tag the runner out.

The shortstop waits between second and third base. The catcher crouches behind home plate. The pitcher throws the ball to the catcher. These two players "talk" using hand signals.

When a catcher puts down two fingers, the pitcher will usually throw a curveball.

The Athletics are an MLB team based in Oakland, California.

Baseball is a worldwide game. Nippon Professional Baseball (NPB) is Japan's top **league**. In the United States, Major League Baseball (MLB) is for pros. Many athletes come from other countries to play in the U.S. Baseball has been part of the Summer **Olympic Games**, too.

league a group of sports clubs that play each other over a period of time for a championship

Olympic Games a set of international sports competitions which take place every four years

Baseball players train with ball drops, bouncing balls against walls, and other drills.

Baseball takes practice.

Hitting a ball with a bat strengthens **hand-eye coordination**. Try this amazing game yourself. Soon you might be knocking it out of the park!

hand-eye coordination the way that one's hands and sight work together to do things that require speed and accuracy

Story of a Player: Ichiro Suzuki

Ichiro

Suzuki grew up in Japan. He joined his first baseball team at age seven. Five years later, he knew he wanted to be a professional baseball player. He was small but dedicated. He threw car tires to gain strength! He became an outfielder for NPB's Orix Blue Wave. Nine years after that, he joined the Seattle Mariners. In 2004, Ichiro set a record for the most hits in one season. Japanese fans flew to the U.S. just to watch him play. Ichiro played MLB into his 40s. In 2018, he began working in the Mariners' front office.

Read More

Bodden, Valerie. *Baseball*. Mankato, Minn.: Creative Education, 2016.

Mason, Tyler. *12 Reasons to Love Baseball*. North Mankato, Minn.: Bookstaves, 2018.

Websites

DK Find Out: Baseball
https://www.dkfindout.com/us/sports/baseball/
Read about the gear used in baseball.

Kiddle: Baseball Facts
https://kids.kiddle.co/Baseball
Learn more about the rules and history of baseball.

Note: Every effort has been made to ensure that the websites listed above are suitable for children, that they have educational value, and that they contain no inappropriate material. However, because of the nature of the Internet, it is impossible to guarantee that these sites will remain active indefinitely or that their contents will not be altered.

Index